Leading Your Child to Christ

Biblical Direction
for Sharing the Gospel

Marty Machowski

New
Growth
Press

www.newgrowthpress.com

New Growth Press, Greensboro, NC 27404
www.newgrowthpress.com
Copyright © 2012 by Covenant Fellowship Church

All Scripture quotations, unless otherwise indicated, are taken from
the *Holy Bible, English Standard Version®* (esv®), copyright © 2000,
2001 by Crossway Bibles, a division of Good News Publishers. Used
by permission. All rights reserved.

Scripture quotations marked niv are taken from the *Holy Bible,
New International Version®*, niv®. Copyright © 1973, 1978, 1984
by International Bible Society. Used by permission of Zondervan. All
rights reserved.

Cover Design: Tandem Creative, Tom Temple, tandemcreative.net
Typesetting: Lisa Parnell, lparnell.com

ISBN-13: 978-1-938267-84-0
ISBN-13: 978-1-938267-30-7 (eBook)

Library of Congress Cataloging-in-Publication Data
Machowski, Martin, 1963–
  Leading your child to Christ : Biblical direction for sharing
the gospel / Marty Machowski.
      p. cm.
  Includes bibliographical references and index.
  ISBN-13: 978-1-938267-84-0 (alk. paper)
  1. Christian education—Home training. 2. Christian education of
children. I. Title.
  BV1590.M33   2012
  268'432—dc23   2012026545

Printed in Canada

20 19 18 17 16 15 14 13   2 3 4 5 6

I remember my dad explaining again to me how Jesus died on the cross for my sins and then rose again after three days. Then my dad helped me to pray, asking God to forgive me of my sins. As I have grown up and gone through children's ministry and now youth ministry, it is exciting to see God revealing himself to me in personal ways not only at those meetings but also in personal devotions and in those around me. — Ruth

When I was around the age of twelve, my family and I were at church. At the end of the message, the speaker was explaining the gospel, and for the first time, God moved me. I remember for the first time having the joy of the Lord in my heart, and I knew I was saved! — Justin

I always believed Jesus came to die on the cross to pay the penalty for the world's sin and that he rose from the dead and offered salvation to all who believed. In reality, all these facts were only in my head and not in my heart. I never thought of Jesus coming to die for me or that I had to surrender my life to him. I went to youth camp for the first time in the summer before eighth grade, and the first night's message about the younger prodigal son making a decision to go back home affected me. That night I fully surrendered my life to God. — Bethany

Reading these testimonies of God's work in the lives of children helps us to remember that God is mighty to save our kids. Leading our children to Christ is a walk of trust, a journey the Holy Spirit wants to join us on. He gives us directions from his Word to help us as we do our best to lead our children to Jesus. And yet, too often we fall out of faith into fear or complacency. Our fears can lead us to try to save our children ourselves, instead of trusting that the Spirit of God is in charge of exactly when and how our children grow in faith. Fear can even lead us to claim our children are converted prematurely or have us give up when we don't see the changes we were hoping for. On the other hand, when we are complacent, we don't take seriously our calling as parents to share the good news of the gospel with our children, preferring to "let go and let God." As always the gospel of Jesus Christ opens up a better way—living the good news of forgiveness for sins in front of our children, actively sharing from God's Word how they can be saved, praying with and for our children, and putting all of our trust in the only One who can grow faith in their hearts (1 Corinthians 3:6).

Often when children make a profession of faith, you have to wait and see what the Spirit is doing in their life. For example, when my daughter Emma was five years old, she responded to a gospel invitation at the end of an evangelistic TV program while we were on vacation. But my wife Lois and I didn't start calling up relatives to announce our daughter's salvation. We knew that it would take time to know if Emma had really accepted Jesus or if that day's experience was one of several events God would use to draw her closer to himself. Still, I must admit, like many parents faced with evaluating a child's response to the gospel, I wrestled a bit and wondered if instead of waiting I should just "have more faith" and believe she was saved.

A couple of years later, at age seven, Emma again prayed in the quiet of her room and has since told us that she went to children's ministry the following Sunday "feeling cool" because she "prayed the prayer." But as the days wore on, and she thought about it more, she realized that nothing in her life had really changed. She didn't enjoy reading the Bible or spending time with the Lord. It wasn't until six years later when she hit the teen years that Emma truly turned away from her sin, and trusted in Jesus. Looking back at her prayer as a seven-year-old, she would now say that she was not a Christian, and she can't even remember the evangelistic TV show she saw when she was five.

My daughter's story is not unique. God is often at work drawing our children to him multiple times prior to their conversion. Yet, parents and others who minister to our children are sometimes too quick to celebrate an early affirmation of the gospel as a full conversion to Christ before they see true change. Later this can cause confusion in the life of a teen who isn't living for God but thinks he is a Christian solely based on the fact that he raised his hand at the end of a meeting. That is what happened to Jay. The following is an excerpt from his story:

> I grew up in a Christian home, went to church every Sunday, attempting to live the way I thought was right. At the age of seven, I prayed the sinner's prayer at a Vacation Bible School and pledged my life to Jesus. In the years that followed, I didn't really know what I was getting into, but I knew that it wasn't what I expected. I knew I wanted something, but I didn't know what it was or where to find it—but I knew it was out there.
>
> It wasn't until seven years later, at my second year at youth camp, that I experienced God. The speaker talked about God's love in dying for our sins upon the cross, and how much we need it. I felt

really moved by this and accepted Christ, this time for real. I made my commitment to Christ so that I could live my life for him, and so I could share my faith and tell other people about the gospel.

Jay's Vacation Bible School teacher and some of the other parents thought he became a Christian back when he was seven and excitedly reported back to his parents that Jay had raised his hand. Jay's parents were glad for his response, but opted to wait and see what God was doing in his life. Jay thought he had pledged his life to Jesus, but it wasn't until God reached down and opened Jay's eyes to see his need personally for the gospel that he was converted and his life began to change.

As Jay's pastor, I got to watch God work from a front-row seat. Prior to camp, Jay was a good kid, but he didn't show much affection for God. After camp, Jay's whole life changed. He turned from his sin and began pursuing God. He and another young man gathered their friends to study the Bible and various Christian books to learn more about God. The fruit of Jay's changed life was easy to see.

While you can't thwart a true conversion by responding cautiously, you can give a child false assurance. All you have to do is ask children if they want to make Jesus their "forever friend" and then tell them they are a Christian if they answer yes. Kids love to respond to our teaching, but that doesn't mean the Spirit of God is touching their lives. There is a whole lot more to the gospel than Jesus becoming our friend. I've counseled many families with struggling teens who believed they were Christians because of a childhood response but now felt no need for the gospel. If they were honest, many would admit that they had never lived for Christ, nor had they experienced affections for the Lord, his Word, or the people of God. We have a lot of kids who are Christians by name, but the Spirit of God has not transformed their lives. Helping them to see their sin and need for Christ is the first step in leading them to genuinely repent and turn their hearts toward Jesus.

That doesn't mean that young children can't become Christians. My wife, Lois, first repented of her sins at age five after her mom shared the gospel with her. Upon hearing the gospel message that day, the Spirit of God convicted her little heart. This is clear in hindsight, but her conversion couldn't be confirmed until her life demonstrated that she was turning away from her sin and living for Jesus. While we pray God will save our children at a young age, and proclaim the gospel from the time they can talk, we should be patient to wait for the changed life that results from genuine repentance, which always flows from the life of a child transformed by the gospel.

You don't need to be a pastor or specially trained to share the gospel effectively with your children. The Bible offers the same gospel to adults and children alike. The introductory stories are true stories. God wants us to have an expectant faith that the powerful gospel can touch the lives of our children. The great preacher, Charles Spurgeon, said it well, "The things that are essential to salvation are so exceedingly simple that no child need sit down in despair of understanding the things which make for his peace. Christ crucified is not a riddle for sages, but a plain truth for plain people. True, it is meat for men, but it is also milk for babes."[1]

Along with the words we share, our example speaks loudly. The effectiveness of the gospel message is confirmed in the minds of our kids when they see it operating in our lives. Whether they see us living for Christ or confessing our sin when we fail, God can use our example to draw them into the kingdom. This is a process that our children see unfolding over time. As they see the gospel change us into kinder, gentler, more patient people, the Spirit uses this to give them hope that God can also change them as they come to him through faith in Jesus. Use the guidelines below to share the gospel with your child, but remember as you share that it is the work of the Spirit to change both you and your child.

Leading Your Children to Christ Is As Easy As A-B-C-D

A - Admit You Are a Sinner Separated from a Holy God

The first step in sharing the gospel with children is to give them a biblical view of their true condition. Children are born sinners, but they don't often think of themselves that way. Consider how often they have heard their parents or other relatives address them as a "good kid." By helping them see the bad news of their sin and separation from God, we help them understand their need for the good news of the gospel.

Sin is not hard to explain to a child—it is simply wanting to be our own god and to live our lives apart from God's rule. So sin is more than just the bad things that we do. Even nice things can be sinful if we do them to get what we want, instead of to please God. Isaiah says that Jesus had to come because "all we like sheep have gone astray; we have turned—every one—to his own way" (Isaiah 53:6). Sin might seem like an abstract concept, but all children can relate to wanting their own way! The bad news is that we are all born wanting our own way, so we are all born sinners. Since the time Adam and Eve decided not to obey God, all of their children (and that includes us) haven't obeyed God either. The Bible explains our condition without Jesus as being dead, because there is nothing we can do to save ourselves (Ephesians 2:5). We can't stop sinning on our own—it's part of our human nature that we inherited from our first parents.

The other half of the bad news for us is that God is holy. God's holiness is his absolute moral purity that compels him to judge and punish sin. The apostle John says that "God is light and in him there is no darkness at all" (1 John 1:5). We need to teach children about God's holiness and that because God is good, he must punish sin. The punishment for sin is death and eternal separation from God forever in hell. "When we understand the character of God, when we grasp something of his holiness, then we begin to understand the radical character of our sin and helplessness. Helpless sinners can only survive by grace."[2] Understanding our sinfulness in the light of God's holiness is what helps us to see our need for deliverance. As sinners who have rebelled against God and gone our own way, we deserve his judgment, but Jesus offers us salvation by taking our punishment upon himself.

Helping our children see their sin in contrast to God's holiness helps them see their problem before God. When you read Bible stories to your child, make sure you explain sin to them in a way that they can understand and relate to. For example, Adam and Eve didn't want to obey; Cain was jealous that his brother was noticed and he wasn't; the Israelites complained in the desert and didn't believe God was going to help them. This opens up a pathway for children to see that the gospel is good news. The word *gospel* actually means good news! It is only when our children are convinced of their sin before a holy God that the gospel sounds like good news to them.

As you share Bible stories, also help your children identify with the sinner in the passage that needs to be rescued. Instead of identifying with David, the young shepherd boy facing the giant Goliath, help them identify with the fearful Israelites standing on the sidelines. God sends David as a savior to deliver Israel. Again and again the message of the Bible points to the love of God in rescuing sinners. We are the sinners; Jesus is the Savior.

As parents, we also need to be convinced about our own sinfulness and need for a Savior. We should be going back to the gospel all the time. While children will learn they are sinners each time we correct them, when they hear us confess our failures too, they get a fuller picture of the pervasive effects of sin. Imagine your child is caught in a sin and you respond in anger. You want to send them to their room for the rest of the day, but instead you admit you were wrong to yell at them, tell them how much you love them and how you remember struggling when you were young in the same ways. While you may still bring them a consequence, it will be more likely seen as care instead of condemnation. We don't want our children to grow up saying they had a mom or dad that never admitted they were wrong. Each time we sin before our children, we have an opportunity to ask for God's forgiveness and use our gospel hope and restoration as a way to demonstrate the promise God extends to them too.

Scriptures for Reference

"Surely I was sinful at birth, sinful from the time my mother conceived me." (Psalm 51:5 NIV)

"As it is written: 'None is righteous, no, not one; no one understands; no one seeks for God. All have turned aside; together they have become worthless; no one does good, not even one.'" (Romans 3:10–12)

"For the wages of sin is death, but the free gift of God is eternal life in Christ Jesus our Lord." (Romans 6:23)

Questions for Reflection

- When was the last time my children heard me confess my own sin and ask their forgiveness, showing them my own need for a Savior?

- How well do I identify with them in their sinful struggles and relate to them that God has helped them in Christ to overcome in the same areas?

B – Believe in Your Heart the Full Gospel of Christ

As soon as we finish sharing the bad news of our separation from a holy God, we move to share the good news of the gospel with our children and call them to believe. Even though believing is a simple concept, what we believe and how we believe are important. As parents, this is where it is so important we share our excitement for all God has done for us. If God comforts or encourages you in your morning devotions or you experience the forgiveness of God for your sin in a fresh way, make sure you share that experience with your children. We are pointing them to a living God, not just a historical story.

Believing requires fully trusting in the complete gospel plan of salvation. Apart from knowing the gospel, you can't believe in the gospel. The gospel has an irreducible core of truth that can't be changed or eliminated.

- God the Father, out of his great love, sent his one and only Son, Jesus, to save his people who, because of their sins, are separated from God and deserving of death.
- Jesus, who is God, humbled himself and took on the nature of a man and led a sinless life.
- Jesus was crucified on the cross unjustly by the hands of men and received the wrath of God upon himself for the sins of all who would believe.
- Jesus was the perfect Lamb of God who took upon himself the sins of the world.
- Jesus acted as our substitute, taking our punishment, so now those who repent and believe in Jesus will live forever with God as their Father.
- Jesus is our Savior who, after taking the full fury of God for our sin, uttered the most wonderful words, "It is finished," and then died and was buried.
- Jesus, on the third day, rose again, showing us his victory over death and sin.
- Jesus is Lord over all creation, and we must submit our lives to his rule.
- Jesus has sent all of his followers into the world to share the good news of repentance and forgiveness of sins.
- Jesus will return one day to take us home to be with him in heaven.

- The Holy Spirit was sent by the Father to help all who trust in Jesus live for him. He changes our hearts and changes the hearts of those we share the gospel with.

It is also important that we teach our children how we believe. The apostle Paul uses the expression "believe in your heart" to describe how we are to believe (Romans 10:9–10). Believing is more than consenting to the truth of the facts of the gospel. James tells us that the demons know the facts about Jesus when he says, "Even the demons believe—and shudder" (James 2:19). But we know that the demons are not going to heaven. Believing is not only knowing, it is completely trusting in Jesus. When our children see us trusting in God through trial, or hear us confess our sin, it gives our faith credibility in their eyes and the Spirit of God uses these moments to work on their young hearts.

We should be careful not to trivialize believing with statements like, "All you have to do is accept Jesus into your heart," or "Just make Jesus your forever friend." Better to use biblical appeals based on scriptures like those in Acts. "Repent therefore, and turn back, that your sins may be blotted out" (Acts 3:19); "I preached that they should repent and turn to God and prove their repentance by their deeds" (Acts 26:20 NIV). Notice these biblical appeals require both faith and repentance.

We shouldn't call children to faith without also calling them to repentance. Repentance from our sin and faith in Christ are a part of the same gospel call. Repentance means to turn away. You are going away from God, but then, by God's grace, you turn away from your sin, toward God. It is true that we grow in our repentance as we are gradually made more like Jesus, but there is a turning from our sin that takes place in our initial response to the gospel. "Any genuine gospel proclamation must include an invitation to make a conscious decision to forsake one's sins and come to Christ in faith, asking Christ for forgiveness of sins. If either the need to repent of sins or the need to trust in Christ for forgiveness is neglected, there is not a full and true proclamation of the gospel."[3]

When you talk to your child about repentance, use everyday examples that will help him or her understand that repentance means to be sorry for your sins against God and other people, but also that you must ask God to help you stop sinning. Since repentance means to change your mind or to turn in a new direction, emphasize to your children that the direction they are going in is what counts. Are they turning toward or away from God?

Remember, it is possible for children to understand the facts of the gospel and even approve of these facts and yet not be a Christian. It is not until a child comes to Christ as Savior and places his or her full trust in the work of Christ that they are saved. This trust is a personal decision of their heart, the very core of their being. We want to be careful that all three are present in a child's life and profession (understanding, approving, and trusting in Christ).

When we realize that genuine saving faith must be accompanied by genuine repentance for sin, it helps us to understand why some preaching of the gospel has such inadequate results today. If there is no mention of the need for repentance, sometimes the gospel message becomes only, "Believe in Jesus Christ and be saved" without any mention of repentance at all. But this watered-down version of the gospel does not ask for a wholehearted commitment to Christ—commitment *to* Christ, if genuine, must include a commitment to turn *from* sin. Preaching the need for faith without repentance is preaching only half of the gospel.[4]

It really helps our children to hear about the work of God in our lives. Sharing how God has helped you repent (turn away) from your sin will encourage your children. Sharing a story where you had to confess to a friend that you gossiped, or lied, and how God is helping you change will help your children see repentance in action.

In addition, the gospel is a hope-filled message. We want to be sure to communicate the same compassion for our child's sins that God demonstrates toward us in our sin. God does not treat us as our sins deserve, but he removes our sin as far away as the east is from the west (Psalm 103:10–12). As adults, the gospel message should continue to affect our hearts. After all, these are incredible truths! When in your personal Bible reading or during a message you are freshly touched by the ongoing work of the Spirit of God, share those moments with your children.

Scriptures for Reference

"Whoever believes in the Son of God has the testimony in himself. Whoever does not believe God has made him a liar, because he has not believed in the testimony that God has borne concerning his Son. And this is the testimony, that God gave us eternal life, and this life is in his Son." (1 John 5:10–11)

"If you confess with your mouth that Jesus is Lord and believe in your heart that God raised him from the dead, you will be saved. For with the heart one believes and is justified, and with the mouth one confesses and is saved. For the Scripture says, 'Everyone who believes in him will not be put to shame.'" (Romans 10:9–11)

Questions for Reflection

- How well am I doing in offering my children the hope of the gospel in the midst of my corrections?

- Where am I most tempted toward bitterness and keeping a record of wrongs regarding my children's behavior?

C – Confess Your Faith in Jesus

Regularly teach your children that those who trust in Christ should tell others about their faith and encourage them to share what God is doing in their lives. But rather than press them for a profession, ask questions about God's activity in their lives such as the following: What do you sense God is doing in your life? Is there something about your life you think God would want you to change? How has God helped you with _____ (whatever your child is currently struggling with—perhaps schoolwork, sports, getting along with a sibling or friend)? What has God done for you? And how has God been helping you to believe? Often talk to your child about how God is helping you place your trust in Jesus in the midst of your own challenges and difficulties. It is important for your children to see that your faith is not limited to one day a week. Many people who long to share their faith with unbelievers forget that they have a captive audience with their own children! You've got a harvest field right in your own living room.

As our children enter the grade school years, we can begin to ask them questions about their application of Scripture such as the following: What is the gospel? Why is the cross important to you? When you read the story of Jesus' death and resurrection, how does it affect you? These kinds of questions mine the depths of their heart without leading them artificially to the "right" answer. Notice also that these questions keep God at the center. Rather than asking a child what they have done, ask them what God has done in them. After all, salvation is the work of the Lord, not man. True believers can sense the presence of God in their lives for Scripture tells us that God pours his Spirit into the heart of everyone who believes as a witness and guarantee of their redemption (Ephesians 1:13–14).

Jesus said, "Everyone who acknowledges me before men, I also will acknowledge before my Father who is in heaven, but whoever denies me before men, I also will deny before my Father who is in heaven" (Matthew 10:32–33). Paul said, "If you confess with your mouth that Jesus is Lord . . . you will be saved" (Romans 10:9). While verses like these encourage us to profess our faith, they have moved some to accept a formulaic repentance for fear that unless a child speak out their profession of faith they will not be saved. We don't need to convince our children to pray a prewritten prayer. Asking good questions is a better approach to drawing them out. "I encourage you not to try to force a confession from the mouth of anyone; for a truly believing heart will bring forth its own confession, without inducement or 'baiting.' Anyone who comes to Jesus cannot help but speak out of that which has filled his heart."[5]

Once your children profess faith in Christ, encourage them to share their faith with others. Evangelizing others is a great test to help us understand what we believe and seeing our children sharing their faith is a great demonstration of the grace of God at work in their lives.

Scriptures for Reference

"Everyone who acknowledges me before men, I also will acknowledge before my Father who is in heaven, but whoever denies me before men, I also will deny before my Father who is in heaven." (Matthew 10:32–33).

"So do not be ashamed to testify about our Lord, or ashamed of me his prisoner. But join with me in suffering for the gospel, by the power of God, who has saved us and called us to a holy life—not because of anything we have done but because of his own purpose and grace." (2 Timothy 1:8–9 NIV).

Questions for Reflection

• When was the last time I shared with my children the story of how God saved me?

• How often do my children see me sharing the gospel message with the people God places in my path?

D ~ Demonstrate the Fruit of Repentance (For You and Your Child)

It is important to teach our children that the gospel always produces fruit in the lives of those who believe. Jesus said we are slaves in our sin but that those the Son sets free are free indeed (John 8:36), and all those he chose he also appointed to bear fruit (John 15:16). Christianity is validated by observable repentance. The great Puritan Thomas Watson said, "True repentance, like nitric acid, eats asunder the iron chain of sin."[6] Our own confessions of sin before our children, where appropriate, help them to see that confession and repentance are a normal part of the Christian life.

Our example will help us teach our children that faith and repentance are gifts from God that are to continue throughout our Christian lives. It is their ongoing presence after conversion which helps a person to know they are a child of God. Assurance comes to us, and those watching us, through the obedience we demonstrate to Jesus Christ. Jesus said, "If you love me, you will keep my commandments" (John 14:15). As C. J. Mahaney points out, "The power of the gospel doesn't end when we're justified. When God declares a sinner righteous, He immediately begins the process of making that sinner more like His Son."[7]

The Bible tells us that we are to forgive others as the Lord has forgiven us. Our free and willing forgiveness of our children sends a powerful message. Imagine if your son or daughter just scratched your car with their bicycle. They expect to receive your anger but instead, when they confess, they experience no wrath, no anger, only forgiveness! That is the power of God at work in you that they can see! Through the work of his Spirit, through the power of his Word, and involvement with the local church, God changes our desires for sin into desires to love God and others, renews our minds, and changes our lives.[8]

As parents, this might be the most difficult point to put into practice. We should remember that our children need the Holy Spirit to work in their lives, or we will press them to just try harder and harder. When God fills us with his Spirit, this true heart change can occur because he places a desire in our hearts to live for him. That is why our example of a repentant life before God is so important. When our children see us sin, repent, and then find grace by the Holy Spirit to change, they are encouraged. Only when we apply the gospel to our own lives, will we be able to communicate this effectively to our children.

The fruit of genuine faith and repentance falls into two categories, the "put offs" and the "put ons" (Ephesians 4:22–24). The "put offs" are the sins we regularly committed as unbelievers apart from Christ: anger, selfishness, jealousy, disrespect of parents, indifference to God's Word, and other such sins. The "put ons" are those marks of grace that grow in the lives of believers as we conform to Christ. The most significant of these marks of grace are those that demonstrate an independent ongoing pursuit of Jesus. When we see our children demonstrate an independent engagement in worship, prayer, Bible reading, and a love for hearing God's Word, that is great evidence that God has given them new life. And when we see our children demonstrate a growing love for others and a desire to serve in community with believers, we can be sure that God is at work in their lives.

So, when do we finally celebrate the conversion of our children? Rather than think, *celebrate conversion*, think, *celebrate the work of grace in their lives*. When Jesus asked the disciples whom did the people say he was, Peter replied, "The Christ, the Son of the living God" (Matthew 16:16). The way that Jesus encouraged Peter is the same way we can encourage our children. Jesus did not say, "Congratulations, Peter, you are a Christian! Let's write this date in your Bible and call up all your relatives!" Jesus' emphasis was on what God did in Peter, not on what Peter did. Jesus said, "Flesh and blood has not revealed this to you, but my Father who is in heaven" (Matthew 16:17).

When we see confession of sin, profession of Christ, or a change in sinful patterns of behavior, we should encourage our children and alert them to the grace of God at work in their lives. At some point, their faith in Christ will become an obvious fact as you regularly encourage them and direct them back to the gospel when they sin. Another wonderful evidence of the grace of God is godly sorrow over their sins. Try not to miss these opportunities to help them acknowledge what God is doing in them. Finally, standing up for Christ in the face of ridicule is a powerful evidence of conversion. When your son or daughter begins sharing the gospel with others and appealing for their repentance, it is likely that the Spirit of the living God has added an ambassador for the King to your family!

Scriptures for Reference

"What good is it, my brothers, if someone says he has faith but does not have works? Can that faith save him? If a brother or sister is poorly clothed and lacking in daily food, and one of you says to them, 'Go in peace, be warmed and filled,' without giving them the things needed for the body, what good is that? So also faith by itself, if it does not have works, is dead." (James 2:14–17)

"And by this we know that we have come to know him, if we keep his commandments. Whoever says 'I know him' but does not keep his commandments is a liar, and the truth is not in him, but whoever keeps his word, in him truly the love of God is perfected. By this we may know that we are in him: whoever says he abides in him ought to walk in the same way in which he walked." (1 John 2:3–6)

"Godly sorrow brings repentance that leads to salvation and leaves no regret, but worldly sorrow brings death. See what this godly sorrow has produced in you: what earnestness, what eagerness to clear yourselves, what indignation, what alarm, what longing, what concern, what readiness to see justice done." (2 Corinthians 7:10–11 NIV)

Questions for Reflection

- How well do I communicate the important role the Holy Spirit plays in helping my children put off their sin and put on affection and obedience toward God?

 Is there an appropriate area of struggle in my life (anger, laziness, jealousy, coveting) that I can share with my children and invite them to watch God work change in me?

The Rest of the Story

As my wife and I began to see evidence of faith in the life of our daughter Emma, we began to believe God had saved her. But it wasn't until we read the following testimony she wrote that we discovered exactly how it happened:

> As I grew older, I started to question whether or not I really was a Christian because I didn't find pleasure in reading the Bible or spending time with the Lord. Around age 13, the evening after hearing a message preached to the youth, I got up in the middle of the night, feeling the weight of my sin. I went into our bathroom and got down on my knees, and I told God that I wouldn't stop praying until he lifted the weight off of my shoulders. I told him that I believed that his Son had come and died for my sins and that if I trusted in him I would have eternal life. I cried and prayed for at least twenty minutes, begging the Lord to save me from my sins.
>
> After I was done praying, I got up, and I was sure that God had forgiven me, a sinner, and that Jesus had died on the cross for my sins, therefore giving me the gift of eternal life. I wanted to go outside and yell out to the whole world that the Lord had died for me and forgiven me of my transgressions. I can now say without a doubt that I am a Christian saved by the grace of God.

My wife and I had no knowledge of Emma's wrestling with God, so it was easy in reading her testimony to realize that we didn't convert our daughter, God did.

Remembering that it is God who saves our children, keeps us from pride and crediting our parenting for their salvation. In the same way, knowing only God can save spares us the condemnation that can affect us when our children continue in their rebellion and are slow to change.

When we understand that our job is to share the gospel, but it is God that does the saving, we can relax, look to do our part, and watch God work. Let's regain the important truth that the gospel is "the power of God" (Romans 1:16) for our salvation. By sharing a clear gospel message each and every week, we can be faithful to the charge of Jesus, who said, "Let the little children come to me and do not hinder them, for to such belongs the kingdom of heaven" (Matthew 19:14).

Endnotes

1. Charles Spurgeon, *Spiritual Parenting* (New Kensington, Penn.: Whitaker House, 2003), 58.

2. R. C. Sproul, *The Holiness of God* (Wheaton, Ill.: Tyndale House Publishers, 1985), 233.

3. Wayne Grudem, *Bible Doctrine*, ed. Jeff Purswell (Grand Rapids, Mich.: Zondervan Publishing House, 1999), 297.

4. Ibid., 312.

5. Dennis Gunderson, *Your Child's Profession of Faith* (Amityville, N.Y.: Calvary Press, 1998), 10.

6. Thomas Watson, *The Doctrine of Repentance* (Carlisle, Penn.: The Banner of Truth Trust, 1999), 52.

7. C. J. Mahaney, *The Cross Centered Life* (Sisters, Oreg.: Multnomah Publishers, 2002), 31.

8. I have paraphrased Mahaney's above-mentioned work, page 31.